Learn the basics of the Turkish language.

Volume 1

Practical methods for learning Turkish

Elie Fiata & Mehmet Güneş

Table of contents

FOREWORD VI

INTRODUCTION VII

1   GRAMMAR 1

  1.1   THE TURKISH ALPHABET 1
    1.1.1   Vowels 1
    1.1.2   Consonants 1
  1.2   TO GREET AND TO THANK IN TURKISH 5
  1.3   THE STRUCTURE OF TURKISH PHRASES 6
    1.3.1   Vowel harmony 7
      1.3.1.1   Simple Vowel harmony with A and E 7
      1.3.1.2   Complex vowel harmony. 8
    1.3.2   Case-endings 11
  1.4   PERSONAL AND POSSESSIVE PRONOUNS 14
  1.5   DEMONSTRATIVE PRONOUNS 17
  1.6   THE ARTICULATIONS IN TURKISH 18
  1.7   VOICELESS CONSONANTS IN TURKISH 18
  1.8   TURKISH CONJUGATION. 21
    1.8.1   The verb to be 21
    1.8.2   The verb to have and not to have 25
    1.8.3   Regular verbs 27
      1.8.3.1   The infinitive form 27
      1.8.3.2   Negation of verbs in Turkish 28
      1.8.3.3   Conjugation 28
        1.8.3.3.1   Indicative 28
      1.8.3.4   The imperative 34
      1.8.3.5   Expressing the possibility 34
      1.8.3.6   How to express: To have to 36
      1.8.3.7   Passive voice of verbs 36
      1.8.3.8   Expressing a need in Turkish 37
      1.8.3.9   Compound verbs 38
  1.9   THE FORMATION OF WORDS IN TURKISH 39
    1.9.1   By reduplication 39
    1.9.2   By composition 39
    1.9.3   By suffix 40
  1.10   ASKING QUESTIONS IN TURKISH 44
    1.10.1   Interrogative adverbs 44

1.10.2 Interrogative particle: mi? (Is it?) 46

1.11 POSTPOSITIONS 47

1.12 COMPARISON 49

2 VOCABULARY 50

2.1 CARDINAL NUMBERS 50

2.1.1 Ordinal numbers 52

2.2 VOCABULARY OF TİME (MONTHS, DAYS AND SEASONS) 53

2.3 TİME 55

2.4 COLORS (RENKLER) AND FİGURES (GEOMETRİK ŞEKİLLER) 55

2.5 İNDEFİNİTE PRONOUNS 56

2.6 SOME LİNKERS 57

2.7 QUANTİFİERS 58

2.8 ADJECTİVES AND THEİR OPPOSİTES 58

2.9 VOCABULARY ON VARİOUS SUBJECTS 59

3 PRACTICE 78

3.1 TEXT: İKİ KARDEŞ 78

3.2 CONVERSATION 79

4 CONCLUSION AND ADVICES 82

Foreword

For each language when we speak, it's like a new life that we live "

In this book, the author gives us the key that opens the door to Turkish culture and language. It allows us to take our first steps in this great journey of learning the Turkish language to achieve perfection.

After several years spent on the island of Northern Cyprus, I observed the different French and English-speaking communities based in North Cyprus, and it was with bitterness that I was able to identify one of the biggest obstacles to social, economic and personal development: *the lack of learning the language which at the same time prevents us from fully integrating ourselves into Turkish society.*

"Thanks to languages, we feel at home anywhere" - Edmund de Waal

Every language you learn is a barrier that you break down, they say. This book gives you the opportunity to tear down those walls that prevent you from integrating into this world which is completely foreign to you. It opens the doors to a fulfilling life in Turkish society.

As students, Businessman or businesswoman or even Tourist, the Author of this book gives you the basics of the Turkish language, allowing you at the same time to no longer feel like a foreigner, isolated or even lost in the Turkish society. With this book, you will no longer have to settle for small jobs that are not up to your skills.

I invite you to discover this gold mine with me.

"Death and life are in the power of the tongue". Proverbs 18:21

Pastor Olivier Bomeki Kasongo

Introduction

The Turkish language is one of the most beautiful languages in the world (in my opinion), both for the beauty of the musicality of its expression and the beauty of the harmony of its writing.

Turkish is, typically, an agglutinating language. It mainly uses suffixes and few prefixes. It is an SOV (subject-object-verb) language. It has a vowel harmony system.[1]

Turkish has no grammatical gender. Thus, nouns, adjectives, participles, pronouns and verbs are totally invariable depending on the gender, they never agree. We do not therefore care whether the word is masculine, feminine or neutral. There is therefore for example only one pronoun of the third person in Turkish to express the English he, she, it and that: o.

Turkish belongs to the "Ural-Altaic" language family, as do Japanese and Hungarian. It is related to Mongolian and happens to be, in fact, an Asian language. It was enriched by Persian and Arabic over the course of historical events, invasions and population movements.

Fortunately for us, since 1928, Turkish has been written using the Latin alphabet. This reform is due to the initiative of Mustafa Kemal who wanted to westernize it, which once again demonstrates his attraction to Europe.

A complete overhaul of the language in 3 months

Beyond the alphabet, the entire Turkish language has been recast. The Ottoman Empire had 5 official languages. Coexisted in

---

[1] Wikipedia. (2020). *Turc*. Available: https://fr.wikipedia.org/wiki/Turc. Last accessed 04th Aug 2020.

particular in the empire Jews from Spain, Greek Orthodox, Persians, Arabs, Levantines of French or Italian origin, and of course Turks from Central Asia. It is from this eclectic people that Ataturk wanted to make a nation, and to unite its citizens, it was necessary to reinvent a single and homogeneous language.

The change was decreed in 3 months but the population took longer to get used to it: only 5% of the citizens were able to read and speak Ataturk's new language! This is how Arabic words gave way to Turkish words and French words (nearly 5,000!) Were introduced.

Today 60 million people speak Turkish. But in fact, 120 million humans speak it (or a derivative) in the Balkans, Asia Minor, northern Iran, all of ex-Soviet Central Asia, Siberia and northeastern Iran. China. Turkish is the 11th most spoken language in the world.[2]

So, get out your notebook and pen, because you are about to learn.

---

[2] Marie, E. (2009). *D'où vient le turc.* Available : https://lepetitjournal.com/istanbul/actualites/langue-dou-vient-le-turc-cette-langue-qui-nous-parait-si-etrange-11211. Last accessed 07th Aug 2020.

1 Grammar

1.1 The Turkish Alphabet

The Turkish alphabet has 29 letters including 8 vowels and 21 consonants.

1.1.1 Vowels

Among the 8 vowels, we have two types of vowels:

Back or hard vowels	Front or soft vowels
A I U O	E İ Ö Ü
They are said to be hard because they are pronounced behind the mouth. Vowels without dots.	These are spoken in front of the mouth. Vowels with dots.

<u>Notice</u>: it is very important to be able to master the two types of vowels and to be able to differentiate them because they are the key point of almost everything in the Turkish language. Pay close attention to it. Get back to it as much as you can.

1.1.2 Consonants

Consonants are 21 in number divided into two categories:

Soft or voiced consonants: b, c, d, g, ğ, j, l, m, n, r, v, y, z
Hard or voiceless consonants: ç, f, h, k, p, s, ş, t

Let's note that the consonants **Q, W** and **X** do not exist in Turkish, and in some words borrowed from other languages, these consonants have been replaced by K (for Q, e.g. Kota instead of

Quota), V (for W, e.g. vagon instead of wagon) and KS (for X, e.g.Taksi or oksijen instead of Taxi and oxygen).

In Turkish, as in English, all letters are pronounced.

Here are all the letters and their pronunciation:

Turkish letters	Pronunciations	Examples
A, a	[a] as in father	**Araba** = car /a-ra-ba/
B, b	[be] as in **b**oy	**Bir** = one, 1 /bi-r/
C, c	[d͡ʒ] as in **j**oy	**Cicim** = sweetie /dʒi-dʒi-m/
Ç, ç	[t͡ʃ] as in **ch**air	**Çiçek** = flower /tʃi-tʃe-k/
D, d	[de] as in **d**og	**Doktör** = doctor /do-k-teu-r /
E, e	[e] as in **r**e**d**	**Televizyon** = TV /te-le-vi-zi-o-n/
F, f	[fe] as in **f**ar	**Fakir** = poor /fa-ki-r/
G, g	[g] as in **g**ot	**Galip** = winner /ga-li-p/
Ğ, ğ	It's called **Yumuşak g** (soft g), it never starts a word and is not pronounced but only lengthens the preceding vowel.	**Sağol** = Thanks /saa-ol/ **Dağ** = mountain /daa/ **Ağaç** = tree /aa-a- t͡ʃ /

H, h	[h] as in **hot**	**Lahana** = cabbage /la-ha-na/ **Merhaba** = Hello /me-r-ha-ba/
İ, i	[i] as in f**ee**t	**iş** = work /i-ʃ /
I, ı	[ɯ] this letter is pronounced between the i and u as in op**e**n	**Kapı** = door /ka-pë/
J, j	[ʒ] as in mea**s**ure	**Ajans** = agency /a- ʒan-s/
K, k	[ke] as in **k**it	**Kalem** = Pen /ka-le-m/
L, l	[le] as in **l**ove	**Bilmek** = to know /bi-l-me-k/
M, m	[m] as in **m**an	**Mavi** = blue /ma-vi/
N, n	[n] as in **n**ice	**İnternet** = internet /i-n-te-r-ne-t/
O, o	[o] as in m**o**re	**Otel** = hotel /o-te-l/
Ö, ö	[œ] as in nurse	**Öğrenci** = student / œ-ren-dʒi/
P, p	[p] as in **p**in	**Parmak** = finger /Pa-r-ma-k/
R, r	[r] in Turkish, we roll the r, it's like a Spanish r and as **tt** in American English	**Radar** = radar /ra-da-r/
S, s	[s] as in **s**ong	**Sormak** = to ask /so-r-ma-k/

Ş, ş	[ʃ] as in **sh**ow	**Lefkoşa** = the city of Lefkoşa /le-f-ko-cha/
T, t	[t] as in **t**oy	**Tuz** = salt /tu-z/
U, u	[u] as in **Zoo**	**Çocuk** = child /tʃo-dʒu-k/
Ü, ü	[û] As ee in feet with lips rounded	**Gün** = jour /gû-n/
V, v	[v] as in **v**at	**Vapur** = Steamboat /va-pour/
Y, y	[y] as in **y**es	**Yemek** = to eat /ye-me-k/
Z, z	[z] as in **Z**igzag	**Zürafa** = giraffe /zû-ra-fa/

• Turkish is read as letters are pronounced in the alphabet.

Practice by trying to read the following words or phrases:

Defter : notebook

sözlük : dictionnary

mutlu : happy

yürek : heart

görecekler : they will see

karşı : against

daha : more

sağlar : provides

köfte : meatballs

kuru : dry

zor : difficult, hard

hedef : goal

çünkü : because

bulacaklar : they will find

temiz : clean

egemenlik : sovereignty

ışık : the light

dünya : world

söylemek : to say

plaj : beach

anne : mother

kitap : book

var : there is   **bu yüzden** : that's why
çabucak : quickly   **kötü** : bad
sevgi : love   **sevinç** : joy
iyilik : kindness   **bağlılık** : commitment
birlik : unity   **Temmuz** : july
honolululuyum : I am from Honolulu
göze göz, dişe diş : eye for an aye, tooth for a tooth
arkaşlarımlayım : I'm with my friends

1.2 To Greet and to Thank in Turkish

Merhaba = hi
Selam = hi

Günaydın = good morning
 iyi günler = good day
Tünaydın = good afternoon
iyi akşamlar = good evening
iyi geçeler = good night
Güle güle = Goodbye (said by the one who stays)
Hoşçakal = Goodbye (said by the one who leaves)
Görüşürüz = see you! (Literally we see each other)

Say Thank you

Sağol, this is the nice thank you, Much more used after certain
wishes like **kolay gelsin** (literally may it come easily) meaning good
luck, work well, ...

Teşekkürler, it's a little more sustained thank you but not really. It is used between friends or strangers to say thank you without showing manners. The quick "Thanks"

Teşekkür ederim is the formal, polite, respectful and can be said to absolutely everyone. Friend, family, boss, stranger. It goes everywhere.

Mersi.

Rica ederim
Bir şey değil   both are for : **you're welcome**

1.3   The structure of Turkish Phrases

In English, the order of words in a sentence is: *Subject-Verb-object* (SVO).

> e.g. My father watches news every morning.

The group of words in the sentence coming before the verb is the subject group and those after the verb are the object group. But this is not the case in Turkish.
The words order in a Turkish sentence is SOV (*subject-object-verb*). This is the formal order of writing but not always respected when speaking)
Let's try to translate the same sentence in Turkish:

> ➤ Benim babam her gün haberleri izliyor.

The verb comes at the end. So how do you know which of the words before the verb is the subject or the object? you might say: well, the first is the subject and the second is the object according to words order in a sentence. You are not wrong. But in other situations, the order of these words can be reversed, or we can have a very long sentence. This is not always obvious.

So, is there any way to find out? YES, of course and it's called **case-endings**. But case-endings and suffixation in Turkish are not done randomly but they follow a very important rule called **vowel harmony.**

1.3.1 Vowel harmony

Vowel harmony is a grammatical system that gives the Turkish language its musicality.

The Turkish language is an **agglutinating** language, which means that words are formed by adding suffixes to other words. And in this chapter, we will learn how to add suffixes to words.

Remember when we talked about the Turkish alphabet, we learned about types of vowels.

Let me jog your memory:

Back (hard) vowels	Front (soft) vowels
A I O U	E İ Ö Ü

There are two types of vowel harmony: simple and complex.

1.3.1.1 *Simple Vowel harmony with A and E*

When adding a suffix, we see the last vowel of the word.

For example, to form the plural of words in Turkish, we add the suffix **lar** or **ler** to the word.

 How to add:

- We add **lar** when the last vowel of the word is a back vowel.

     e.g. çocuk = çocuk**lar** (children)

BACK – LAR   FRONT – LER

Telefon = telefon**lar** (phones)
Baş = baş**lar** (heads)
Kapı = kapı**lar** (doors)

- We add the suffix **ler,** when the last vowel is a front vowel.
  e.g. ev = ev**ler** (houses)
       Söz = söz**ler** (words)
       Gün = gün**ler** (days)
       Defter = defter**ler** (notebooks)

Practice by putting the following words in plural:

Dağ (mountain) =	Yol (chemin) =
Ögrenci (student) =	Hastane (hospital) =
Devlet (stat) =	Ülke (country) =
Bayrak (flag) =	Koşul (condition) =
Şarkı (sing) =	Yatak (bed) =
Söz (word, promise) =	Göz (eye) =
Masa (table) =	Ders (lesson) =
Pencere (window) =	Yumurta (oeuf) =
Hesap (account) =	Mutfak (cuisine) =

1.3.1.2 *Complex vowel harmony.*
(It's complex, pay close attention and practice as much as you can to master it)

We have two types of vowels:

Back vowels   and   Front vowels
   A I O U   E İ Ö Ü

Among these categories, there are other sub-categories

Sub-categories	Back vowels	Front vowels
Unrounded	A	E
	I	İ
Rounded	O	Ö
	U	Ü

For example: to form adjectives from nouns, we add the suffixes **lı /
li / lu / lü**

- we add the suffix **lı**, when the word's last vowel is a **back-unrounded** vowel.

> e.g. yaş (age) = yaş**lı** (old)
> Hız (speed) = hız**lı** (fast)

- We add the suffix **li**, when the last vowel of the word is a **front-unrounded** vowel.

> e.g. güneş (sun) = güneş**li** (sunny)
> Önem (importance) = önem**li** (important)
> Resim (image) = resim**li** (illustrated)

- We add the suffix **lu**, when the last vowel of the word is a **back rounded** vowel.

> e.g. bulut (cloud) = bulut**lu** (cloudy)
> Tuz (salt) = Tuz**lu** (salty)
> Limon (lemon) = limon**lu** (based on lemon)

- We add the suffix **lü**, when the last vowel of the word is a soft rounded vowel.

> e.g. süt (milk) = süt**lü** (in or with milk)
> Söz (speech) = söz**lü** (verbal)
> İkigöz (two faces) = ikigöz**lü** (hypocrite)

Summary tables

Simple Vowel harmony

A I O U	-a
E İ Ö Ü	-e

Complex vowel harmony

A I O U	I U
E İ Ö Ü	İ Ü

Note: whenever we have a suffix in which there is an **a** or **e**, the suffix will be added according to *the simple vowel harmony*.

Each time we have a suffix in which there is an **i** or **u**, the suffix will be added according to *the complex vowel harmony*.

Practice by forming adjectives from following words

Akıl (intelligence) =
Hak (right) =
Güç (power, strength) =
Fark (difference) =
Kir (dirt) =
Paha (cost) =
Sağlık (health) =

Muz (banana) =
Hareket (movement) =
Ün (fame) =
Nem (humidity) =
Gurur (pride) =
Rüzgar (wind) =

Having learned how to add suffixes to words in Turkish, let's now learn what case-endings are.

1.3.2 Case-endings

Case-endings are a morphological change in nouns that determines the function they play in a sentence.

There are cases; Turkish has 6 (Fortunately! because there are languages that have more, even up to 18).

Case	Functions	Suffixes
Nominative or Absolute case	We use this case when the word in the sentence is **subject**.	**No suffix**. The word keeps its absolute form. e.g. *Baba* ailenin başıdır (the father is the head of the family)
Accusative	We use this case when the word in the sentence is a **direct object**	**(y)i/ı/ü/u** e.g. herkesi seviyorum (I love everyone)
Genitive	We use this case when the word in the sentence indicates ownership or expresses a possession (the English 's)	**(n)in** e.g. Baba aile**nin** başıdır (the father is the head of the family = the family's head)
Locative	When the word indicates a current situation. Where someone or something is (**in, at**)	**da/de** okul**da**yım (I'm at school) ev**de** misin? (are you at home?)
Dative	when the word indicates a direction. Where	**(y)e/a** ev**e** gidiyorum (I'm going to home

	someone or something points to (**to**) when the word is an **indirect object**	çocuklar okul**a** gidiyor (children are going **to** school) para**yı** anneme Verdi (he gave money to my mother)
Ablative	When the word indicates an origin. Where someone or something comes from. (**from**)	**Dan/den** Okul**dan** geliyorum (I'm coming from school)

Notes:

- Case-endings are added to nouns according to **vowel harmony**.
- Suffixes are separated from proper names by an apostrophe.

e.g. *Yarın Turkiye'ye gidecek* = He will go to Turkey tomorrow.
Elijah'ın çantası çok seviyorum = I really like Elijah's bag.

- To express the time, we use the locative case:

e.g. *Akşam saat dokuz**da** (9'da) geleceğim* = I will come at 9 p.m.
*Saat beş**de** (5'de) okula gideceksiniz* = you will go to school at 5

- We can add multiple suffixes to a word at the same time. The case-endings suffixes are added in last position.
e.g. çantalarımı kaybettim (I lost my bags) = accusative

Now that we know what case-endings are and how they work (give nouns their functions in a sentence) according to vowel harmony, let's practice together:

(Recall the order of the words in a sentence: SOV).

- Ev**den** (*ablative*) restoran**a** (*dative*) gitmek için geldim = I came from home to go to a restaurant.

 - babam (*nominative*) iş adamlar**ı** (*accusative*) sever = my father likes businessmen.

- Usta (*nominative*) askerlerin**e** (*dative*) dedi ki: kalk ve savaş**a** (dative) git = the master says to his soldiers: get up and go to war.

- asker**in** (*genitive*) karısı hasta = the soldier's wife is sick

- İstanbul Türkiye'**de** (*locatif*) bir şehir = Istanbul is a city in Turkey

- Öğrenciler (*nominative*) okumay**ı** (*accusative*) ve yazmay**ı** (*accusative*) öğrenir = students learn to read and write.

- yeni bir dil (*nominative*) öğrenmek biz**e** (*dative*) kapılar**ı** (*accusative*) açar = a new language to learn (learning a new language) opens doors to us (for us).

- Ev**e** (*dative*) gelirsen okul**a** (*dative*) gideceğiz = if you go home, we will go to school
- Ev (*nominative*) satıldı = the house has been sold

Ev**i** (*accusative*) aldık = we bought the house

Ev**in** (*genitive*) bahçesi = the garden of the house

Ev**de** (*locative*) kaldı = he stayed at home

Ev**den** (*ablative*) uzak = it's far from home

Hasan'**ı** (acc) hemem tanıdım = I immediately recognized Hasan

1.4 Personal and possessive pronouns

Personal and possessive pronouns take case-endings in Turkish and they change in form and meaning.

Case	1st P. sing	2nd P. s	3rd P. s	1st P. plural	2nd P. p	3rd P. p
Nominative	**Ben** = I	**Sen** = you	**O** = he/she/it	**Biz** = we	**Siz** = you	**Onlar** = they
Accusative	**Beni** = me	**Seni** = you	**Onu** = him / her	**Bizi** = us	**Sizi** = you	**Onları** = them
Genitive	**Benim** = my	**Senin** = your	**Onun** = his / her	**Bizim** = our	**Sizin** = your	**Onların** = their
Dative	**Bana** = to me	**Sana** = to you	**Ona** = to him / to her	**Bize** = to us	**Size** = to you	**Onlara** = to them
Ablative	**Benden** = from me	**Senden** = from you	**Ondan** = from him / her	**Bizden** = from us	**Sizden** = from you	**Onlardan** = from them
Locative	**Bende** = on/in me	**Sende** = in you	**Onda** = on/in him	**bizde**	**sizde**	**onlarda**

❖ In Turkish, the use of personal pronouns as subject (**in nominative case**) is not necessary. They are used to reinforce or clarify the subject. (the verb determines the subject)

> e.g. seni seviyorum (I love you)
>   Her gün Ekmeği yerim (I eat bread every day)

Yarın gideceğiz (we will leave tomorrow)
Dört kitabı günde okurlar (they read 2 books a day)

❖ The use of personal pronouns as direct object (**in accusative case**) is mandatory and comes after the subject (if there has).

Ex: **seni** seviyorum (I love you = I love you)
Annem **Beni** bekliyor (my mother is waiting for me)
onları buraya getir (bring them here)

❖ The use of possessive adjectives (**in genitive**) is not necessary. They are used just to reinforce the idea of possession.

But we add suffixes to express possession in Turkish.

How to express possession:

- Benim… - **(i/ı/ü/u)m** {the vowels in parentheses, this is in case the word ends in a consonant and according to vowel harmony}

- Senin… - **(i/ı/ü/u)n**

- Onun… - **(s)i/ı/ü/u** {le (s) in case the word ends in a vowel}

- Bizim… - **(i/ı /ü /u)miz**

- Sizin… - **(i/ı/ü/u)niz**

- Onlarin… - **(s)i/ı/ü/u** or **(lar / ler)i/ı/ü/u**

Examples: baba (father) and kalem (pen)

(benim) baba**m** (my father)   Kalem**im** (my pen)
(Senin) baba**n** (your father)   kalem**in** (your pen)
(onun) baba**sı** (his father)   kalem**i** (his pen)
(bizim) baba**mız** (our father)   kalem**imiz** (our pen)

(sizim) babanız (your father)   kaleminiz (your pen)
(onların) babası (their father)   kalemi (their pen)

Babalarım (my fathers)   kalemlerim (my pens)
Babaların (your fathers)   kalemlerin (your pens)
Babaları (his fathers)   kalemleri (his pens)
Babalarımız (our fathers)   kalemlerimiz (our pens)
Babalarınız (your fathers)   kalemleriniz (your pens)
Babaları (their fathers)   kalemlerı (their pens)

onun telephonu (his telephone)
Hayatım (my life)   çantam (my bag)
gözlerüm (my eyes)   arkadaşımız (our friend)
onların annesi (their mother)   onların anneleri (their mothers)

bilgisayarımı kaybettim (I lost my computer)
hoşgeldiniz evimize! (welcome to our house)
sizin üniversitenizin kapılar mavi (your university's doors are blue)

❖ Personal pronouns in **dative** are used to express direction or an
   indirect object.

   e.g. **bana** gel (come to me)
        onlara git (go to them)
bize ekmeğimizi gündelik ver = give us (give to us) our daily bread
bana bakıyordu (he was looking towards / at me)
sana tesekkür ederim (I thank you)

❖ Personal pronouns with **ablative** mark an origin (coming from
   the speaker).

e.g. kardeşine **benden** selam söyle = say Hello to your brother for me (from me).

❖ Personal pronouns in locative also mark a place.
e.g. bu gömlek **sizde** var mı? (Is there this shirt on you?)

1.5 Demonstrative pronouns

There are three demonstrative pronouns in Turkish:

Singular	plural
Bu> this	**Bunlar**>these,
Şu> this	**Şunlar**> those,
O> that	**Onlar**> those,

Examples:

Bu benim babam:	This is my father
Şu annem	This is my mother
Şunlar sizin evleriniz	These are your houses.
O çocuk sizinki mi?	Is this child yours?
O çocuklar güzel	These children are beautiful.
bu benim evim	This is my house
bu restoran uzak	This restaurant is far
bu elmalar lezzetli	These apples are delicious
şu yıldızlar parlak	These stars are bright

1.6 The articulations in Turkish.

In Turkish, there is no article.

Often, **bir** is used as an indefinite article:

> Ex: dışarıda **bir** araba var (there is **a** car outside)

But sometimes, when speaking of a very specific object and very determined, that we need to use a definite article in Turkish.

We add the suffix **(s) i/ı/ü/u** to place a definite article before the word or to form compound nouns:

> e.g. Kara deniz**i** = the black sea
>
> Yatak oda**sı** = the bedroom
>
> Kibris illim üniversite**si** = Cyprus University of Science
>
> Otobüs durağ**ı** = the bus station
>
> Uçak bilet**i** = the plane ticket
>
> Mutfak kapı**sı** = the kitchen door
>
> Doğum günü hediye**si** = birthday present
>
> Bilgisayar uzman**ı** = computer specialist (computer scientist)

1.7 voiceless consonants in Turkish

Remember that we have two types of consonants, soft (voiced) consonants and hard (voiceless) consonants. Voiceless consonants have a certain particularity.

Here are all the voiceless consonants: **ç, f, h, k, p, s, ş, t.**

Here is a sentence to easily remember them: **Fa PaŞa ÇoK HaSTa**

The Turkish language is a musical language, voiceless consonants are switched into other voiced consonants when adding suffixes to words.

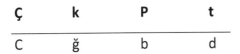

The 4 voiceless consonants above are switchable into voiced consonants below or vice versa. But the 4 others are not permutable (**F, Ş, H, S**)

1. *When a word ends with a **voiceless** consonant and the suffix you want to add begins with a vowel, then the voiceless consonant of the word is swapped by its corresponding.*

e.g. çocuk (to say my child, the k changes and becomes ğ + the possessive suffix of the first person singular) = çocuğum

(Kitap) kıta**b**ımız = our book / kita**b**ım - My book

(dolap) Dola**b**a koydum - I put it in the closet (*dative*)

(ağaç) Ağa**c**a bak - Look at the tree (*dative*)

(borç) Bor**c**um ne kadar? - how much is my debt?

(Yoğurt) Hakan yoğur**d**u yedi - Hakan ate the yogurt (*accusative*)

(Dört) Saat dör**d**e çeyrek var - It's a quarter to four (*dative*)

(Sözlük) İngilizce-Türkçe sözlü**ğ**ün var mı? - Do you have an English-Turkish dictionary? (*possession*)

(çocuk) Fatih çocu**ğ**a şeker verdi - Fatih gave candy to the child

(Kalp) benim kal**b**ım seni seviyor - my Heart loves you.

(Genç) henüz genciz - we are still young
Gitmek (to go): git + iyorum = gidiyorum (I'm leaving)
etmek (to do): et + eriz = ederiz (we do)

<u>Note</u>: The letter "k" is replaced by a "**g**" instead of a "**ğ**"when it has an "n" in front of it and a vowel after it:

(renk) Göz ren**g**i - Eye color
(kepenk) Ömer kepen**g**i kapattı - Ömer closed the shutter

<u>Exercise</u>: say

Bardak (glass): .... (My glass)

Ayak (foot): .... (His foot)

Çiçek (flower): .... (Your flower)

İhtiyaç (need): .... (Our need)

Amaç (objective): .... (their objective)

2. *But when the suffix we want to add begins with a consonant, then the consonant of the suffix is swapped (if possible) and the voiceless consonant of the word remains.*

e.g. çocuk (to say I was a child, the consonant of the suffix (dum) will be permuted by its correspondent) = çocuk**tum** (I was a child)

(Kapatmak) kapıları kapat**tik** = we closed the doors (past tense)
(Park) Park**tay**ız = we are at the Park (*locative*)
(Park) Park**tan** geliyorlar = they come from the Park (*ablative*)
Türk (a Turkish) + ce (to form languages) = türk**çe** (Turkish)
Hafif (light) + ce (to form adverbs) = hafif**çe** (lightly)

1.8 Turkish conjugation.

Conjugation, as in all languages of the world, remains a crucial and somewhat complicated part of grammar in a language, as each language has its own rules.

Conjugation in the Turkish language can be a bit confusing, because it uses a suffix system (which is not always easy to master) but it is still an important part that you have to be able to understand if you want to speak the Turkish language clearly.

1.8.1 The verb to be

The verb to be is the only auxiliary verb in Turkish, and it is conjugated by attaching to the word (except for the future tense).

The infinitive form of the verb to be is Olmak (which can also mean to become, to happen ...)

> e.g. Avukat olmak istiyorum = I want to be (become) a lawyer.
> Ne oluyor? Ne oldu? = what's going on? what happened?

1. Present

Affirmative

negative

- (y) **im** = I am
- **Sin** = you are -
- **(dir)** = he is -
- (y) **iz** = we are -
- **Siniz** = you are -
- **(lar / ler)** = they are -

- **degilim** = I am not
- **değilsin** = you are not
- **değil** = he / she is not
- **değiliz** = we are not
- **değilsiniz** you are not
- **değiller** = they are not

22

Note:

- The verb to be is conjugated as a suffix in Turkish and it is used according to vowel harmony. So, it may be **im/ım/um/üm** (for all other person it's the same)

- For the first person singular and plural, we add **"y"** when the word ends with a vowel

- For the 3rd person of singular, the suffix **"dir"** is optional. It is often used in quotes or to reinforce or emphasize the person.

- The negative form is not used as a suffix.

Examples:

- Genç (young) + im = genc**im** (I am young)
- Güzel (beautiful, pretty) + im = güzel**im** (I'm handsome, pretty)
- Çocuk (child) + um = çocuğ**um** (I am a child)
- Deli (crazy) + sin = deli**sin** (you are crazy)
- Bu kız kötü(**dür**) = this girl is bad.
- Bu su = it's water
- Kardeş (brother) + iz = Kardeş**iz** (we are brothers)
- Hasta (sick) + sınız = hasta**sınız** (you are sick)
- Yorgun (tired) + uz = yorgun**uz** (we are tired)
- Postacı (factor) + lar = postacı**lar** (they are factors)
- Üzgün (sorry, sad) + üm = üzgün**üm** (I'm sorry, sad)
- Kızgın (angry) + sınız = kızgın**sınız** (you are angry)
- Rahat (comfortable) + ız = rahat**ız** (we are comfortable.)
- Rahatsız (uncomfortable) + ım = rahatsız**ım** (I am uncomfortable)
- Çocuklar güzel**ler** = children are beautiful

Negative

- Genç değil + im = genç değil**im** (I'm not young)
- Hasta değil + sin = hasta değil**sin** (you are not sick)
- Kardeş değil + iz = kardeş değil**iz** (we are not brother)
- Meşgul değil + ler = meşgul değil**ler** (they are not busy)
- Bu kız kötü değil = this girl is not bad.
- Rahat değil + siniz = rahat değil**siniz** (you are not comfortable)
- Mutlu değil + iz = mutlu değil**iz** (we are not happy)
- Emin değil + im = emin değil**im** (I'm not sure)
- Bu ilişki ciddi değil = this relationship is not serious

2. The past

Affirmative		Negative	
(y)dim	I've been/was	**değildim**	
(y)din		**değildin**	
(y)di		**değildi**	
y)dik		**değildik**	
(y)diniz		**değildiniz**	
(y)diler		**değildiler**	

The (**y**) is in case the word ends in a vowel.

3. The future

Affirmative	Negative
- **Olacağım** = I will be	**Olmayacağım** = I will not be
- **Olacaksın**	**Olmayacaksın**
- **Olacak**	**Olmayacak**
- **Olacağız**	**Olmayacağız**
- **Olacaksınız**	**Olmayacaksınız**
- **Olacaklar**	**Olmayacaklar**

Examples: past and future

- Genç**tim** (ç being a hard vowel, the d becomes t)
- Güzel**dim** (I was beautiful)
- Hasta**ydınız** (you were sick)
- Meşgül değil**dim** (I have been busy)
- Deli değil**diler** (they weren't crazy)
- Öğretmen **olacağım** (I will be a teacher)
- Öğrenci**ydimiz** (we were students)
- Fakir **olamayacağız** (we will not be poor)
- Yetim değil**diler** = they were not orphans.
- Çocuk**tum** = I was a child.
- Çocuklarım çiçek **olacaklar** = my children will be flowers.
- Fakir **olmayacaksin**, zengin **olacaksin** = you won't be poor you will be rich

Practice with the person and time of your choice
Samimi (sincere) =
Hırslı (ambitious) =
Akıllı (intelligent) =
Güclü (strong) =
Yalnız (alone) =
Adam (man) =
Üzgün (sad)
iyi (good, good) =
kızgın (angry) =

[Don't forget the vowel harmony, in this case it's the complex vowel harmony]

First, learn how to express things, situations or emotions in present, past and future. Other tenses will come with time.

1.8.2 The verb to have and not to have

The verb to have does not exist in Turkish.

But to express ideas of possession or not possession, we use VAR (which literally means there is) and YOK (there is not)

How it works.
Var and Yok walk with possession

> **Noun + possession suffix (of the person according to vowel harmony) + var / yok**

Notes: the subject goes to the genitive case.

To say for example: *I have a pen.*
We will say: (**benim**) bir (a/one) **kalem** (pen) -**im** (my) **var** (there is)
Bir kalemim var = I have a pen

Bir kalem**in** var = you have a pen
Bir kalem**i** var = he / she has a pen
bir kalem var = there is a pen (without any possession suffix)
Bir kalem**imiz** var = we have a pen
Bir kalem**iniz** var = you have a pen
kalemler**i** var = they have pens
onun üç küçük köpeği var = he has three little dogs
sevecen bir baba**m** var = I have a loving father
hiç kıtab**ımız** yok = we don't have any book
Para**m** yok = I don't have money

Onların Onlarda Televizyonu yok = They don't have a television at home.
Annemin ateşi var = my mother has a fever
Arkadaşımın güzel bir arabası var = my friend has a nice car
defterimin kapağı yok = my notebook has no cover.

Past: **Vardı / Yoktu**

Bir köpeğim vardı ama öldü = I had a dog but he died

bugün hiç dersim yoktu (I had no lessons today)

baska çarem yoktu (I had no other choice)

uykum vardı (I was sleepy)

Practice:

I have a mother: ………………………………………………

You had a sister: ………………………………………….

We had money but now we don't have money:
………………………………………………………………

My father has two wives: ………………………………………………………

Girls have phones these days:
………………………………………………………………

1.8.3 Regular verbs

1.8.3.1 The infinitive form

The infinitive forms in Turkish are **mek** or **mak**

Some common verbs in Turkish

Gelmek	To Come	**Yüzmek**	To swim
Gitmek	To Go	**Yemek**	To eat
Girmek	To Enter	**Hissetmek**	To feel
Sevmek	To Love	**Çizmek**	To draw
Açmak	To Open	**Ögretmek**	To teach
Koymak	To put	**Ögrenmek**	To learn
Bırakmak	To leave	**Sormak**	To ask
Duymak	To hear	**Planlamak**	To plan
Bilmek	To know	**Istemek**	To want
Ölmek	To die	**Parlamak**	To shine
Dönmek	To return	**Dokunmak**	To Touch
Uyumak	To sleep	**Uyanmak**	To wake up
Almak	To receive, to take, to buy	**Yemek yapmak**	To Cook
Dinlenmek	To have a rest	**Cevap vermek**	To answer
Dinlemek	To listen	**Açıklamak**	To explain
Kapatmak	To close	**Evlenmek**	To get married
Koşmak	To run	**Kullanmak**	To use
Hatırlamak	To remember	**Izlemek**	To watch
Bakmak	To look, to take care of	**Yapmak**	To Make
Okumak	To Reading	**Yazmak**	To Write
Çalışmak	To work	**Konuşmak**	To talk
Teşekkür etmek	To Thank	**Demek / söylemek**	To Say / to tell
Düşünmek	To Think	**Içmek**	To drink
Oturmak	To sit	**Başlamak**	To start
kıpırdamak	To move	**yüzmek**	To swim

28

But There are also nouns ending in mek or mak which are not verbs and should not be confused with verbs.

Ex: ekmek = bread.

Parmak = the finger

1.8.3.2 *Negation of verbs in Turkish*

Negation of verbs in Turkish is done using the suffixes: **me / ma** (according to vowel harmony)

> **The verb stem + me / ma + infinitive form**

- Okumak (to read) = oku (stem) + **ma** (negation) + **mak** (infinitive) = okumamak (not to read)
- Bilmek (to know) = bil + me + mek = bilmemek (not to know)
- Almak (to take) = almamak (not to take)
- Gözmek (see) = gözmemek (not to see)

e.g. okuyorum = I read

Okumuyorum = I don't read

Biliyorum = I know

Bilmiyorum = I don't know

1.8.3.3 *Conjugation*

1.8.3.3.1 Indicative

1. Present tense

The indicative mode has two present tenses as in English: simple (present of the habit) and the present continuous ((present of the action, of the moment)

e.g. Her gün iki ekmeği **yerim** (I eat two loaves of bread every day)
Ekmeği **yiyorum** (I am eating bread)

Verbs follow vowel harmony. And we'll talk a lot about a verb stem. It simply is the verb without its infinitive form (the verb without mek or mak: gitmek = git (the stem))

A. <u>Simple present</u>: To conjugate verbs in simple present:

- When the verb stem ends with a vowel:

verb stem + **r** + the person's suffix

	Demek To say	anlamak to understand	korumak to protect
	Der**im**	Anlar**ım**	Korur**um**
	Der**sin**	Anlar**sın**	Korur**sun**
	Der	Anlar	Korur
	Der**iz**	Anlar**ız**	Korur**uz**
	Der**siniz**	Anlar**sınız**	Korur**sunuz**
	Der**ler**	Anlar**lar**	Korur**lar**
	I say	I understand	I protect

- When the verb stem ends with a consonant:
  - When the verb stem is a monosyllable:

Verb stem + a/e + r + the person's suffix

Binmek : To get on	Yapmak : to do	Dönmek : to get back	Sunmak : to present
Binerim	Yaparım	Dönerim	Sunarım
Binersin	Yaparsın	Dönersin	Sunarsın
Biner	Yapar	Döner	Sunar
Bineriz	Yaparız	Döneriz	Sunarız
Binersiniz	Yaparsınız	Dönersiniz	Sunarsınız
Binerler	Yaparlar	Dönerler	Sunarlar

But for this rule, there are 13 exceptions (13 verbs whose stems are monosyllables and ending with a consonant but get conjugated according to the next rule (like verbs whose stems are polysyllabic). These 13 verbs are:

Almak (take, buy, receive), **gelmek** (come), **vermek** (give), **varmak** (to arrive), **olmak** (become, happen, be), **bulmak** (find), **durmak** (stop), **görmek** (see), **vurmak** (to strike), **bilmek** (to know), **ölmek** (to die), **kalmak** (to stay), **sanmak** (to assume)

- When the verb stem is a polysyllable:

Verb stem + **i/ı/u/ü** + **r** + the person's suffix

İmrenmek : To Covet	aldatmak to deceive	konuşmak : to speak	süpürmek to sweep
İmrenirim	Aldatırım	Konuşurum	Süpürürüm
İmrenirsin	Aldatırsın	Konuşursun	Süpürürsün
İmrenir	Aldatır	Konuşur	Süpürür
İmreniriz	Aldatırız	Konuşuruz	Süpürürüz
İmrenirsiniz	Aldatırsınız	Konuşursunuz	Süpürürsünüz
İmrenirler	Aldatırlar	konuşurlar	Süpürürler

B. Present continuous

To conjugate any verb in present continuous tense:

Verb stem **+ i/ı/u/ü + yor** + person suffix

- When the verb stem ends with a consonant, one of the vowels in the formula is added (according to vowel harmony) then we add **yor**
  e.g. gelmek = geliyor (he is coming)

- When the verb stem ends with one of the vowels in the formula, there is no need to add another one, we add **yor** directly.
  e.g. okumak = okuyor (he is reading)

- When the verb stem ends with a vowel other than those appearing in the formula, the vowel is deleted and is replaced by one of the vowels that appear in the formula, according to vowel harmony.
  e.g. dinlemek = dinl(e)iyor = dinliyor (he's listening)

Almak : To take	Gelmek : to come	Görmek : to see	Bulmak : to find
Alıyorum	Geliyorum	Görüyorum	Buluyorum
Alıyorsun	Geliyorsun	Görüyorsun	Buluyorsun
Alıyor	Geliyor	Görüyor	Buluyor
Alıyoruz	Geliyoruz	Görüyoruz	Buluyoruz
Alıyorsunuz	Geliyorsunuz	Görüyorsunuz	Buluyorsunuz
Alıyorlar	Geliyorlar	Görüyorlar	Buluyorlar

Choose verbs from the table of common verbs in Turkish and conjugate them in order to practice.

2. The past tense

A. The simple past

To conjugate verbs in the past simple:

> Verb stem + **di/dı/du/dü** + person suffixes

Almak :   Gelmek :   Görmek :   Bulmak :
To take   to come   to see   to find

Al**dım**	Gel**dim**	Gör**düm**	Bul**dum**
Al**dın**	Gel**din**	Gör**dün**	Bul**dun**
Al**dı**	Gel**di**	Gör**dü**	Bul**du**
Al**dık**	Gel**dik**	Gör**dük**	Bul**duk**
Al**dınız**	Gel**diniz**	Gör**dünüz**	Bul**dunuz**
Al**dılar**	Gel**diler**	Gör**düler**	Bul**dular**

I took / I've taken ...

B. Past continuous

To conjugate any verb in the past continuous:

> Verb stem + + **i/ı/u/ü** + **yor** + **du** + person suffixes

Almak :   Gelmek :   Görmek :   Bulmak :
To take   to come   to see   to find

Al**ıyordum**	Gel**iyordum**	Gör**üyordum**	Bul**uyordum**
Al**ıyordun**	Gel**iyordun**	Gör**üyordun**	Bul**uyordun**
Al**ıyordu**	Gel**iyordu**	Gör**üyordu**	Bul**uyordu**
Al**ıyorduk**	Gel**iyorduk**	Gör**üyorduk**	Bul**uyorduk**
Al**ıyordunuz**	Gel**iyordunuz**	Gör**üyordunuz**	Bul**uyordunuz**
Al**ıyordular**	Gel**iyordular**	Gör**üyordular**	Bul**uyordular**

I was taking

1. Futur tense
A. Futur simple
to conjugate any verb in futur simple:

verb Stem + (y)acak/ecek + person suffixes

Başlamak : To start	Gelmek : to come	Görmek : to see	Bulmak : to find
Başlayacağım	Geleceğim	Göreceğim	Bulacağım
Başlayacaksın	Geleceksin	Göreceksin	bulacaksın
Başlayacak	Gelecek	Görecek	Bulacak
Başlayacağız	Geleceğiz	Görgeceğiz	Bulacağız
Başlayacaksınız	Geleceksiniz	Göreceksiniz	Bulacaksınız
başlayacaklar	gelecekler	görecekler	bulacaklar

I will start

B. Conditional tense
To conjugate verbs in conditional tense:

Verb stem + (y)acak/ecek + ti + person suffixes

Başlamak : To start	Gelmek : to come	Görmek : to see	Bulmak : to find
Başlayacaktım	Gelecektim	Görecektim	Bulacaktım
Başlayacaktın	Gelecektin	Görecektin	Bulacaktın
Başlayacaktı	Gelecekti	Görecekti	Bulacaktı
Başlayacaktık	Gelecektik	Görecektik	Bulacaktık
Başlayacaktınız	Gelecektiniz	Görecektiniz	Bulacaktınız
Başlayacaktılar	Gelecektiler	Görecektiler	Bulacaktılar

I would start   I would come   I would see   I would find

1.8.3.4 *The imperative*

As in English, the imperative of the 2nd person singular in Turkish is formed by removing the suffix from the infinitive (gitmek = git), but also in Turkish, there are 6-person imperative instead of 3 as in English. And we can add the personal pronoun if we want.

Almak: take   Gelmek: Come

al**ayım**	Let me take	gel**eyim**	Let me go
Al	Take	Gel	Go
Al**sın**	Let him take	Gel**sin**	Let him go
Al**alım**	Let's take	Gel**elim**	Let's go
Alın	Take	Gel**in**	Go
al**sınlar**	Let them take	Gel**sinler**	Let them go

Görmek :   Bulmak :
To see   to find

Gör**eyim**	Let me see	bul**ayım**	Let me find
Gör	See	Bul	Find
Gör**sün**	Let him see	**Bulsun**	Let him find
Gör**elim**	Let's see	**Bulalım**	Let's find
Görün	See	**Bulun**	Find
Gör**sünler**	Let them see	**Bulsunlar**	Let them find

1.8.3.5 *Expressing the possibility*

In French or in English, the possibility and the permission are expressed by the modal verb Can. In Turkish, the possibility is expressed:

The infinitive of can in Turkish: yapabilmek

- For the affirmative form

Verb stem + **abilir/ebilir** + person suffixes

Almak : To take	Gelmek : to come	Görmek : to see	Bulmak : to find
Alabilirim	Gelebilirim	Görebilirim	Bulabilirim
Alablirsin	Gelebilirsin	Görebilirsin	Bulabilirsin
Alabilir	Gelebilir	Görebilir	Bulabilir
Alabiliriz	Gelebiliriz	Görebiliriz	Bulabiliriz
Alabilirsiniz	Gelebilirsiniz	Görebilirsiniz	Bulabilirsiniz
alabilirler	gelebilirler	Görebilirler	bulabilirler
I can take	I can come	I can see	I can find

- for the negative form:

Verb stem + **ama(z)/eme(z)** + person suffixes

Almak : To take	Gelmek : to come	Görmek : to see	Bulmak : to find
Alamam	Gelemem	Göremem	Bulamam
Alamazsın	Gelemezsin	Göremezsin	Bulamazsın
Alamaz	Gelemez	Göremez	Bulamaz
Alamayız	Gelemeyiz	Göremeyiz	Bulamayız
Alamazsınız	Gelemezsiniz	Göremezsiniz	Bulamazsınız
alamazlar	Gelemezler	Göremezler	Bulamazlar
I can't take	I can't come	I can't see	I can't find

1.8.3.6 *How to express: To have to*

> Verb in infinitive **zorunda** + person suffixes

Gitmek : to go

Gitmek zorunday**ım**	I have to go
Gitmek zorunda**sın**	You have to go
Gitmek zorunda	He/she has to go
Gitmek zorunda**yız**	We have to go
Gitmek zoruda**sınız**	You have to go
Gitmek zorunda**lar**	They have to go

For all verbs, it is expressed this way:
Açım, yemek zorundayım (I'm hungry, I have to eat)

1.8.3.7 *Passive voice of verbs*

- If the verb stem ends with a consonant (except "l"), we add to the stem the suffix **"-il"** (according to vowel harmony, it can also be "-**ül", "-ıl" or "-ul"**).

Ex: Yapmak [to do] → Yapılmak [to be done].
Sevmek [to love] → Sevilmek [to be loved]

- If the verb stem ends with "l", we add to the stem the suffix **"-in"**
Ex: Bilmek [to know] → Bilinmek [to be known].

- If the stem of the verb ends with a vowel, we add to the stem the suffix "-n"
Ex: Okumak [read] → Okunmak [be read]

37

We add the adverb "**tarafından**" ("by" in English) after the agent complement (and not before as in English).

e.g. Bu kitap, Elie **tarafından** yazıldı [This book was written by Elie].

The adverb "tarafından" changes according to the person:
Tarafımdan [by me], tarafından [by you], tarafından [by him / her], tarafımızdan [by us], tarafınızdan [by you], taraflarından [by them].

1.8.3.8 _Expressing a need in Turkish_

İhtiyaç (need)
İhtiyacım (my need) **ihtiyacım** var (my need there is = I need)
İhtiyacın (your need), **ihtiyacın** var (you need)
İhtiyacı (his need), **ihtiyacı** var (he needs)
İhtiyacımız (our need), **ihtiyacımız** var (we need)
İhtiyacınız var (you need), **ihtiyaçları** var (they need)

Note: 1. For the negation, we put **YOK** instead of var.
2. **İhtiyaç** requires its subject in _genitive_ and its object in _dative_.

e.g. **Sana** (_dative_) ihtiyacım var = I need you.
Bana ihtiyacın var (you need me)

Sevgiye ihtiyacımız var, Nefrete ihtiyacımız yok (we need love, we don't need hate)

Hayatta birbirimize ihtiyacımız var. herkes önemlidir (we need each other in life. Everyone is important)

Babamın artık hizmetlerine ihtiyacı yok (my father no longer needs your services)

1.8.3.9 _Compound verbs_
In Turkish, some verbs are formed by putting two words together:

Tesekkür etmek (thanks +to do) = to thank
Özür delemek (excuse + to wish) = to apologize
Dikkat etmek (attention + to do) = to be careful
Cevap vermek (answer + to give) = to answer
Tebrikler etmek (congratulations + to do) = to congratulate
Yemek yapmak (meal + to do) = to cook
Söz vermek (word + to give) = to promise
İtaat etmek (obedience + to do) = to obey
Rahatsız etmek (uncomfortable + to do) = to disturb
Ziyaret etmek (visit + do) = to visit
Yemin etmek (oath + to do) = to swear
Kontrol etmek (control + to do) = to verify
İman etmek (faith + to do) = to believe
Dezenfekte etmek = to disinfect
Devam etmek = to continue
Kabul etmek = to accept
Teslim etmek = to deliver
İptal etmek = to cancel

1.9 The formation of words in Turkish

Word formation in Turkish is done in several ways:

- By word reduplication
- By composition
- By suffixation

1.9.1 By reduplication

In Turkish, you can double the same word to form another:

e.g. yavaş (slow) = yavaş yavaş (slowly)
Çabuk (fast) = çabuk çabuk (quickly)
Tatlı tatlı (soft + soft) "gently, very gently"
Güzel güzel (pretty + pretty) "nicely"
Küçük küçük (small + small) "in small pieces"
Sabah sabah (morning + morning) "early, in the morning"
Ayrı ayrı (separate + separate) "separately"
Akşam akşam (evening + evening) "late, in the middle of the evening"

1.9.2 By composition

In Turkish, two words can be put together to form another:

babaanne (father + mother) "paternal grandmother"

açıkgöz (open + eye) "smart"

göz doktoru (eye + doctor) "oculist"

başkent (head + city) "capital"

sonbahar (last + spring) "autumn"

ikiyüzlü (two + face + with) "hypocrite"

1.9.3 By suffix

Most Turkish words are formed this way.

We will see the majority of suffixes, not all of them but the most important ones, because the goal is not to learn all the Turkish grammar but to help you get the basics necessary to express yourself in Turkish.

Suffixes in Turkish

The addition of Turkish suffixes is done according to the vowel harmony.

- **Cik/cık/cuk/cük** to form the diminutive of words (the "c" becomes "ç" after a voiceless consonant)

kuvaför**cük**	"little" hairdresser
Ali'**cik**	Ali "darling"
Şezlong**cuk**	"small" deckchair
Kapıcık	"little" door
Çocukçuk	"little" child
Kitapçık	"little" book
Paris'çik	"little" Paris
Yoğurtçuk	"little" yogurt
Babaçık	"Daddy".

- **Lar or ler**, to form the plural of words:

El (hand) = el**ler** (the hands)
Yatak (bed) = yatak**lar** (the beds)
İnsan (person) = insan**lar** (people)
Göz (eye) = göz**ler** (eyes)
Kulak (ear) = kulak**lar** (ears)
Işık (light) = ışık**lar** (the lights)

bina(building) = bina**lar** (buildings)

But also, to express wishes in Turkish:

İyi (mutlu) + word + lar/ler

İyi gün**ler** = have a nice day
İyi aksam**lar** = good evening
İyi şans**lar** = good luck
Mutlu yıl**lar** = happy new year
İyi pazar**lar** = good Sunday
İyi yolculuk**lar** = have a good trip

- **Ca / Ce** (çe/ça after a voiceless consonant):

1. To form the names of languages:

Fransız (a French) = fransiz**ca** (French)
Türk (a Turk) = türk**çe** (Turkish)
Alman (a German) = alman**ca** (German)
Arap (an Arab) = arap**ça** (Arabic)
İspanyol (a Spanish person) = İspanyol**ca** (Spanish)
İngiliz (an English person) = İngiliz**ce** (English)

2. To form adverbs from adjectives:

Gizli (secret) = gizli**ce** (secretly)
Güzel (pretty) = güzel**ce** (nicely)
Doğru (right) = doğru**ca** (directly)
Hafif (light) = hafif**çe** (lightly)

3. To express an indefinite period "during, for"

Yıllar (years) = yıllarca (for years)
Saatler (hours) = saatlerce (for hours)
Günler (days) = günlerce (for days)

- **ci / cı / cu / cü** (ç after a voiceless consonant) to form the names of the professions:

Taksi (taxi) = Taksi**ci** (taximan)
Öğren (to learn) = öğren**ci** (learner, student)
Çiçek (flower) = çiçek**çi** (florist)
Satı (sale) = satı**cı** (seller)
Savaş (war) = savaş**çı** (Warrior)
Yol (road) = yol**cu** (passenger)
İş (work, employment) = İş**çi** (employee)

- **İnci / ıncı / üncü / uncu** to form ordinal numeral adjectives.

İki (two) = iki**nci** (second)
On (ten) = on**uncu** (tenth)
Üç (three) = üç**üncü** (third)
Altı (six) = altı**ncı** (sixth)

- **Lik / lık / luk / lük**, to form names from names

Mutlu (happy) = mutlu**luk** (happiness)
Çocuk (child) = çocuk**luk** (childhood)
Genç (young) = genç**lik** (youth
Güvensiz (safe month) = güvensiz**lik** (mistrust, insecurity)
Kral (king) = kral**lık** (kingdom)
Yolcu (passenger) = yolcu**luk** (travel)

Evli (married) = evli**lik** (marriage)
Kardeş (friend) = kardeş**lik** (fraternity)
Baba (dad) = baba**lık** (fatherhood)
Kim (who) = kim**lik** (identity)
Var (there is) = var**lık** (presence)
Yok (there is not) = yok**luk** (absence)

- **Li / lı / lu / lü**: to form adjectives from nouns (can be translated literally in French as "with").

Şerker (sugar) = şeker**li** (sweet)
Tuz (salt) = Tuz**lu** (salty)
Süt (milk) = Süt**lü** (in milk or milk
Süphe (doubt) = süphe**li** (with doubt, doubtful)
Güven (trust) = güven**li** = (safe, reliable)
Paha (cost) = paha**lı** (expensive, expensive)

- **Siz / sız / suz / süz**: to form adjectives (in the private sense or the opposite) the suffix can be translated into French as "sans".

Son (last, end) = son**suz** (endless, infinite)
        e.g. Sonsuz bir aşk = an endless love
Süphe (doubt) = süphe**siz** (doubtless)
Koşul (condition) = koşul**suz** (unconditional)
Ölüm (death) = ölüm**süz** (without death, immortal)
Güç (power) = güç**süz** (powerless, weak)
Tuz (salt) = tuz**suz** (without salt)
Şeker (sugar) = şeker**siz** (without sugar)
Tat (taste) = tat**sız** (tasteless)

- **le / la** (+ suffix mek / mak) to form verbs from nouns or adjectives

Baş (head) = baş**la**mak "to start"
Kilit (locked) = Kilit**le**mek "lock"
Kir (dirt) = kir**le**mek "to dirty"
Temiz (clean) = temiz**le**mek "to clean"
buz (ice) = buz**la**mak (to freeze)
zayıf "thin" zayıf**la**mak (to slim down)
ter (perspiration) = ter**le**mek (to perspire)
kira (location) = kira**la**mak (to rent)
Plan (plan) = plan**la**mak (plan)

- **(y) le / la**: with, by (by means of) or ile

Araba**yla** = with the car, by car
Uçak**la** geldi = he came by plane
Benim**le** gel = come with me
Arkadaşlarım**la**yım = I am with my friends
Aile**yle** = with the family
Telefon**la** = by phone, with the phone

Or we can also say:

Araba **ile** = with the car, by car
Uçak **ile** geldi = he came by plane
Benim **ile** gel = come with me

1.10 <u>Asking questions in Turkish</u>

1.10.1<u>Interrogative adverbs</u>

Kim = who
Ne = what

Neden = why
Ne zaman = when
Kaç: how much
Hangi: what
Nasıl : How

Nere / where

- -de = **nerede**: for the situation where we are.
  e.g. Mehmet nerede? where is mehmet?
  Neredesin? Where are you?

- -ye = **nereye**: for the place where you're going.
  e.g. Nereye gidiyorsun? where are you going?

- -den = **nereden**: for the place where one comes from
  e.g. Nereden geliyorsun? where do you come from?

Examples:

Kimsiniz? Who are you?

kim geldi? Who came?

Ne zaman gideceksin? When will you go?

Bu ekmek kaç para? How much does this bread cost?

Hangi parayla? With what money?

Ne içmek istiyorsun? What do you want to drink?

1.10.2 Interrogative particle: mi? (Is it?)

Interrogates the word or the sentence which precedes it, is written separately and conforms to the vowel harmony; mi, mı, mü, mu, and the person suffixes that follow it:

Miyim ? mıyım? Müyüm? Muyum?	Am I?
Misiin? Mısın? Müsün? Musun?	Are you?
Mi? Mı? Mü? Mu?	Is he/she/it?
Miyiz? Mıyız? Müyüz? Muyuz?	Are e?
Misiniz? Mısınız? Müsünüz? Musunuz?	Are you?
Mi? Mı? Mü? Mu?	Are they?

Ahmet **mi**? Is it Ahmet?

Fransız **mı**? Is he / she French?

Geliyor **mu**? Is he (she) coming?

Büyük **mü**? Is he tall?

Öğrenci **misin**? Are you a student?

Hasta **mı**? Is he sick?

Türk **müyüz**? Are we Turkish?

Fransızlar **mı**? Are they French?

İyisiniz (affirmative sentence) You are well.

İyi **mi**siniz? (Interrogative sentence) Are you well?

Türkçe biliyoruz (we speak Turkish)

Türkçe biliyor **mu**yuz?

Geliyorsunuz (you come)

Benim evime geliyor **mu**sunuz? Are you coming to my place?

1.11 Postpositions

In Turkish, there is no preposition; prepositions are placed after the words they introduce and are therefore called POSTPOSITIONS.

We will not be able to see all the postpositions that there are in Turkish, I will suggest a few, find more as you learn:

About: **hakkında**

Across: **karşısında**

Against: **karşısında**

Around: **etrafında**

To: ... **da (de)**.

Behind: **arkasında**

Under: **altında**

Beyond: **ötesinde**

By: **tarafından**

Down: **aşağı**

Except: **dışında**

From: **itibaren**

Inside: **içinde**

Next: **sonra, sonrasında**

On: **üzerinde**

Outside: **dışarı**

More: **artı, ek olarak**

Around: **etrafında**

Through: **sayesinde**, ...

above: **yukarısında**

after: **sonra**

between: **arasında**

like: **gibi**

before: **önce, önünde**

below: **aşağısında**

next to: **yanında**

since: **beri,**

despite: **rağmen**

over: **sırasında**

for: **için**

in: **içinde**

near: **yakın, yakınında**

of: ... **nın**

opposite: **karşısında**

outside: **dışında, dışarısında**

with: **ile**

Without: **olmadan**

Note: postpositions (not all of them) require specific case-endings for the names they determine.

Examples of some sentences:

1. Postpositions requiring the genitive

Sen**in için** bir hediyem var = I have a present for you
masa**nın üstünde** = above the table (on the table)
ağac**ın altında** = under the tree
benim ile gel = come with me
bu adam **benim gibi** = this man is like me

2. Postpositions requiring the dative

Radyo**'ya göre,** bugün hava güzel olacak: according to the radio, the weather will be nice today (it will be nice today)

Hangi takım**a karsı** oynıyacaksınız? (which team will you play against?)

Köy**e kadar** yürüdük (we walked to the village)
Akşam**a kadar** konuştuk (we talked until the evening)

3. Postpositions requiring the ablative

Toplantı**dan sonra**, gitti: after the meeting he left
Nisan**dan beri**: since April

There are several other postpositions that require case-endings.

1.12 Comparison

Positive	Comparative	Superlative
Büyük = big	**daha büyük** = bigger	**en büyük** = biggest
Küçük = small	**daha küçük** = smaller	**en küçük** = smallest
Hızlı = fast	**daha hızlı** = faster	**en hızlı** = fastest
Kolay = easy	**daha kolay** = easier	**en kolay** = easiest
iyi = good	**daha iyi** = better	**en iyi** = best
genç = young	**daha genç** = younger	**en genç** = youngest

How it works

Türk dili ögrenmek **kolay** değil (learning the Turkish language is not easy: positive)

Türkçe Fransızca**dan** daha kolay (Turkish is easier than French)

Note: the object of the comparison is in nominative-case and the compared in ablative-case (**dan** means here: "than")

Ben sen**den** daha inceyim (I'm thinner than you)
Ben sen**den** daha az inceyim (I'm less thin than you)
Annem seninkin**den** daha güzel (my mother is more beautiful than yours)
İspanyolca dünyanın **en** güzel dilidir (Spanish is the most beautiful in the world: superlative

Lucas benim **en** iyi arkadaşım (Lucas is my best friend)

2 Vocabulary

2.1 Cardinal numbers

Tip: master from 1 to 9 and the tens and voila.

sıfır	0	yirmi	20
bir	1	Yirmi bir	21
iki	2	Yirmi iki	22
üç	3	Yirmi üç	23
dört	4	Otuz	30
beş	5	Kırk	40
altı	6	Elli	50
yedi	7	Altmış	60
sekiz	8	Yetmiş	70
dokuz	9	Seksen	80
On	10	Doksan	90
On bir	11	Yüz	100
On iki	12	Yüz bir	101
On üç	13	Yüz on	110
On dört	14	Yüz yirmi	120
on beş	15	Yüz elli beş	155
On altı	16	İki yüz	200
on yedi	17	bin	1000
On sekiz	18	milyon	1000000
On dokuz	19	Bir Milyar	1000000000

Practice with the following numbers:

1) 35 = …………………………………
2) 77 = …………………………………
3) 61 = …………………………………

4) 99 = ...
5) 187 = ...
6) 106 = ...
7) 194 = ...
8) 506 = ...
9) 947 = ...
10) 1806 = ...
11) 64727 = ...
12) 25924 = ...
13) 1583365 = ...
14) 684137 = ...
15) 231465876 = ...
16) 8026931482 = ...

N.B: Numbers in Turkish do not modify words. They never put the words they refer to in plural.

Ex: iki el = two hands (never iki el**ler**)

Beş çantam var = I have 5 bags (never beş çanta**lar**ım var).

Practice translating the following sentences:

a) 18 pens =

b) 5 glasses =

c) let's buy 10 loaves of bread =

d) 20 shirts =

e) 100 cars =

Arithmetic signs:

Artı (plus), **eksi** (minus), **çarpı** (multiplied by), **bölü** (divided by)

Ex: beş **artı** altı on bir eder (five plus six is eleven)
   Yedi **eksi** üç dört eder (7-3 = 4)
   Dokuz **çarpı** beş kırk beş eder (9 multiplied by 5 = 45)
   On **bölü** iki beş eder (10 divided by 2 is 5)

2.1.1 Ordinal numbers

As we have seen in word formation, to form ordinal numbers, we add the suffix *(i)nci* to the numbers, while respecting vowel harmony.
The **(i)** in case the number ends in a consonant.

Birinci = first	**Sekizinci** = eighth
ikinci = second	**Dokuzuncu** = ninth
Üçüncü = third	**Onuncu** = tenth
Dördüncü = fourth	**On birinci** = eleventh
Besinci = fifth	**Elli besinci** = fifty fifth
Altıncı = sixth	
Yedinci = seventh	
Dokuz yüz doksan dokuzuncu = 999th	
Bininci = 1000th	

Grouping

birer birer = one by one

ikişer ikişer = two by two

üçer üçer = three by three

dörder dörder = four by four

beşer beşer = five by five

altışar altışar = six by six

yedişer yedişer = seven by seven

sekizer sekizer = eight by eight

dokuzar dokuzar = nine by nine

2.2 vocabulary of time (months, days and seasons)

Ocak	January	Pazartesi	Monday
Şubat	February	Salı	Tuesday
Mart	March	Çarşamba	Wednesday
Nisan	April	Perşembe	Thursday
Mayıs	May	Cuma	Friday
Haziran	June	Cumartesi	Saturday
Temmuz	July	Pazar	Sunday
Ağustos	August		
Eylül	September	Gün	Day
Ekim	October	Gece	Night
Kasım	November	Dün	Yesterday
Aralık	December	Bugün	Today
		Yarın	Tomorrow
İlkBahar	Spring	Hafta	Week
Yaz	Summer	Ay	Month
Sonbahar	Autumn	Yıl	Year
kış	Winters	Gecen	Last, past
		Gelecek	Next
Sanye	Second	Şimdi	Now
Dakika	Minute	Sonra	Later
Saat	Hour	Önce	Earlier
Hergün	Everyday	hiçbir zaman	Never
Hemen	Right now,	Eskiden	In the old days
Her zaman	Always	Erken	Early
Yakında	Soon	Yılyüz	Century

54

e.g.   *Bugün 2 agustos 2020* (Today is August 2, 2020)

ne kadar zamandır Kıbrıs'tasın? (How long have you been in Cyprus)
2019'dan beri kıbrıs'tayım (I have been in Cyprus since 2019)

Benim dogüm günüm ... (my birthday is ...)

10 yıl sonra eve geldi. (He came home, after 10 years)

yarın plaja gideceğim. (I'll go to the beach tomorrow)

Hava nasıl?	What weather is it?	Güneş	Sun
Sıcak.	Hot.	Gökyüzü	Sky
Soğuk.	Cold.	Hava	Air
		Rüzgar	Wind
yağıyor.	It is raining.	fırtına	Storm
Kar yağıyor	It's snowing.	Bulut	Cloud
		Şimşek	Lightning
Dolu yağıyor.	It hails	Gök gürültüsü	Thunder
Sisli.	Misty.	Kasırga	Hurricane
Bulutlu.	Cloudy.	Sis	Fog
Güneşli.	Sunny.	Yağmur	Rain
Rüzgarlı.	Windy.	Kar	Snow
___ derece.	___ degrees.	Buz	Ice

Hava çok sicak yazda. (It is very hot in summer)

Hava çok güzel baharda. (It's nice in spring)

Sonhabarda çok rüzgâr var. (There is a lot of wind in Autumn)

Geçen kış çok soğuktu. (It was very hot last summer)

2.3 Time

Saat kaç?	What time is it?	Saat tam 5 yönünde.	It's 5 a.m. sharp
Saat 1.	It is 1 o'clock.	gece yarısı.	Midnight
Saat 2.	It's 2 o'clock	Saat sabah 9.	It's 9 a.m.
Saat 3 buçuk.	It is half past three.	Sabah	Morning
		öğle	Midday
Saat 5'i çeyrek geçiyor.	It is quarter past five.	öğleden sonra	Afternoon
6'ya çeyrek var.	It is quarter to 6.	akşam	Evening
Saat 7:12.	It's 7.12	Gece	Night

2.4 Colors (Renkler) and figures (geometrik şekiller)

Ak	White (Turkish origin)	açık	Clear
Beyaz	White (Arab origin).		
Gümüş	Silver	Karanlık	Dark
Altın	Golden	Kutu	box
Kara	Black (Turkish origin)	kare	square
Siyah	Black (Persian origin)		

Gri	Grey	Daire	circle
Mavi	Blue	Küre	sphere
Yeşil	Green	Üçgen	triangle
Sarı	Yellow	Piramit	pyramid
Kırmızı	Red	Dikdörtgen	rectangle
Kahverengi	Brown	Küp	cube
Pembe	Pink Color	Koni	cone
Turuncu	Orange	Altıgen	hexagon
Mor	Purple	Sekizgen	octagon

Notes:

- For white and black, Beyaz and Sihay are the most used.

- The names of the colors come before the words that they qualify as qualifying adjectives.

e.g. *favorite rengin ne*? (What is your favorite color) ?
   Favorite rengim Beyaz. (My favorite color is white)
   gökkuşağı 7 renkleri var? (The rainbow has 7 colors)
   mavi bir şapkam var (I have a blue hat)
   beyaz bir gömeleğim var (I have a white shirt)
   küçük yeşil bir evim var (I have a little green house).

2.5 indefinite pronouns

birisi	someone	Hiç kimse	No one
bir şey	Something	hiçbir şey	Nothing
bir yerde	Somewhere	Hiçbir yerde	Nowhere
herhangi bir şey	Whatever, anything	Herkes	Everybody

herhangi bir yer	Anywhere	**Herşey**	All, everything
istediğin zaman	At any time	**Her yerde**	everywhere
		Her kimse	Anyone

Bir şey diyeceğim (I will say something)

ağır bir yük taşıyan birini gördüm (I saw someone carrying a heavy burden)

kız kardeşimle bir yerdeyim (I'm somewhere with my sister)

Herkes temiz bir kıbrıs için (everyone for a clean Cyprus)

hiçbir yere gitme (don't go anywhere)

kimseyi selamlama (do not greet anyone)

2.6 some linkers

ve	And
Veya (ya da)	Or
Ama	But
Çünkü	Because
Eğer	Si
bu nedenle	So

Sen ve ben (you and I)

Ben siyahım ama güzelim (I am black but I am beautiful)

gelirsin ya da gelmezsin (you come or you don't come)

Evet veya Hayır (yes or no)

Eğer Barış istiyorsun, savaş için hazırlan (if you see peace, prepare for war)

2.7 Quantifiers

Biraz	A little
Çok	A lot
Her	Each
Az	Little
çok	Very
Yeter	Enough
diğer	Other
Birkaç	Some
Bütün	Whole
aynı	Same

birçok arkadaşım var (I have a lot of friends)

Ben biraz türkçe Konuşuyorum (I speak a little Turkish)

her gün markete gidiyorum (every day I go to the market)

Yemek için yeterince sebzem var (I have enough vegetables for the meal)

2.8 Adjectives and their opposites

Büyük	Big tall	Küçük	Small
Şişman	Fat	Sıska	Skinny
Geniş	Tall, wide	Dar	Narrow
Güzel	Beautiful	Çirkin	Ugly
Temiz	Clean	Kirli	Dirty
Sessiz	Quiet	Gürültülü	Noisy
Hızlı	Quick	Yavaş	Slow
Tam	Full	Boş	Empty
Soğuk	Cold	Sıcak	Hot

Açık	Open	Kapalı	Closed
Aynı	same	Farklı	Different
Erken	Early	Geç	Late
Akıllı	Clever	Aptal	Idiot
Uzun	Long	Kısa	Short
Genç	Young	Yaşlı	Old
Mutlu	Happy	Üzgün	Sad
Daha	More	Az	Little
Yeni	New	Eski	Former

2.9 vocabulary on various subjects

Transport and places

Uçak	Plane	Avlu	Court
Otomobil	Car		
Bisiklet	Bike	Kuru temizlemeciler	Dry cleaners
Tekne	Boat	Elçilik	Embassy
Otobüs	Bus	Fabrika	Factory
Araba	Car	Çiftlik	Closed
Motosiklet	Motorbike	Garaj	Garage
Gemi	Ship	Bakkal	Grocer
metro	Subway	Hastane	Hospital
Taksi	Taxi	Otel	Hotel
Tren	Train	Ev	House
Kamyon	A truck	Kütüphane	Library
Havalimanı	Airport	Market	Market
Fırın	Bakery	Anıt	Monument

Banka	Bank	Müze	Museum
Bar	Bar	Saray	Palace
Ahır	Barn	Pastahane	Pastry
Bank	Bench	Eczane	Pharmacy
Kitapçı	Bookstore	Polis Merkezi	Police station
Bina	Building	Postane	Post office
köprü	Bridge	Restoran	Restaurant
Kasap	Butcher	Okul	school
Kale	Castle	Stadyum	Stadium
Katedral	Cathedral	Mağaza	Shop
Mezar	Tomb	kenar mahalle	Suburbs
Mezarlık	Graveyard	Tiyatro	Theater
Kilise	The church	Kule	Tower
Sinema	Cinema	Belediye binası	Town hall
Konsolosluk	Consular	Üniversite	University
Köşe	Corner	Kasaba	City

Familly

Dede	Grandfather	Nene	Grandmother
babaanne	Grand-mother	anneanne	Maternal grandmother
Baba (ata)	Dad	Anne (ana)	Mom
Koca, eş	Husband, husband	Karı , eş	Wife
Erkek (adam)	Man	Kadın	Women
Erkek kardeş	brother	Kız kardeş	Sister
Oğlan	boy	kız	girl

Oğul	son	kız	girl
Abi	Big Brother	abla	Older sister
Erkek arkadaş	friend	Kız arkadaş	girlfriend
Arkadaş	friend	Komşu	Neighbor
Çocuk (lar)	Child (ren)	Bebek	Baby
Erkek yeğen	Nephew	Kız yeğen	niece
Erkek kuzen	cousin	Kız kuzen	cousin
amca	Paternal uncle	Hala	Paternal aunt
Dayı	Maternal uncle	Teyze	Maternal aunt
erkek torun	Grandson	kız torun	granddaughter
ikiz(ler)	Twin (x)	Evli	Married
boşanmış	Divorcee	Nişanlı	Fiancé
dul	Widower widow	Hamile	pregnant
bekâr	single		

The parts of the human body (Vücut parçaları)

Kan	Blood	Kalp	Heart
Kemik	Bone	Kafatası	skull
Beyin	Brain	Cilt	Skin
Nefes	Breath	Omuz	Shoulder
Çene	Chin	Kaburga	Rib
yanak	Play	avuç içi	Palm
sakız	Gum	İncik	Shank

Alın	Forehead	**Boyun**	Neck
Yumruk	punch	**Burun**	Nose
Kol	Arms	**Dudak**	Lip
ayak bileği	Ankle	**Ağız**	Mouth
Karın	Abdomen	**Bacak**	leg
Arka	Back	**Diz**	knee
Göğüs	chest	**Kalça**	Hip
Kaş	eyebrow	**Topuk**	Heel
göz kapağı	Eyelid	**Çene**	Chin
Yüz	Face	**Omurga**	spine
parmak	Finger	**Mide**	Stomach
Göz	Eye	**Boğaz**	Throat
ayak (ayaklar)	Foot (s)	**Başparmak**	Thumb
Dirsek	Elbow	**ayak parmağı**	toe
Kulak	Hear	**Dil**	Language
Saç	Hair	**diş (dişler)**	Tooth (s)
El	Hand	**Bel**	Cut
Baş	Head	**Bilek**	wrist

Fruits and vegetables

Badem	Almond	**Enginar**	Artichoke
Fındık	Hazelnut	**Sarımsak**	Garlic
Greyfurt	Grapefruit	**Ot**	Cannabis
Kayısı	Apricot	**Kuşkonmaz**	Asparagus
Avokado	Lawyer	**Arpa**	Barley

Muz	Banana	**Fasulye**	Beans
Yabanmersini	Blueberries	**Brokoli**	Broccoli
Karpuz	Watermelon	**Çilek**	Strawberry
Turp	Radish	**Domates**	Tomato
Lahana	Cabbage	**Kereviz**	Celery
Kaşu	Cashew	**Frenk soğanı**	Chive
Kiraz	Cherry	**Mısır**	But
Kestane	Chestnut	**Salatalık**	Cucumber
kuş üzümü	Currant	**patlıcan**	Eggplant
Meyve	Fruit	**Pırasa**	Leek
elma	Apple	**Mercimek**	Lens
buğday	Corn	**Marul**	Salad
Havuç	Carrot	**Nane**	Mint
Yaprak	Leaf	**Mantar**	Mushrooms
Limon	Lemon	**Yulaf**	Oats
Kavun	Melon	**Soğan**	Onion
Zeytin	Olive	**Maydanoz**	Parsley
Şeftali	Peach	**Bezelye**	Peas
Armut	Pear	**Patates**	Potato
Portakal	Orange	**Kabak**	Pumpkin
Ananas	Pineapple	**Turp**	Radish
Fıstık	Peanut	**Pirinç**	Rice
Erik	Plum	**Çavdar**	Rye

Home and supplies (ev ve malzemeleri)

Alarm	The alarm	**Ev**	The House
Banyo	The bathroom	**zemin kat**	The ground floor
Küvet	The bathtub	**Bahçe**	The garden

Cd oynatıcısı	CD player	**Mutfak**	The kitchen
Apartman	The apartment	**Lamba**	The lamp
Koltuk	The armchair	**Çim**	The lawn
çatı katı	The attic	**mektup kutusu**	The letter box
Balkon	The balcony	**Şilte**	The mattress
Bodrum	The basement	**Ayna**	The mirror
Perde	The curtain	**Fırın**	The oven
Ofis	Office	**mikrodalga fırın**	The microwave oven
yemek odası	The dining room	**halı**	The carpet
Garaj	The garage	**Yaprak**	The sheet
Mobilya	The furniture	**Tuvalet**	Toilet
Mağaza	The shop	**Duvar**	The wall
Yatak	The bed	**pencere**	The window
yatak odası	Bedroom	**ekmek kızartma makinesi**	The toaster
Kapak	The blanket	**Televizyon**	Television
Yastık	The cushion	**Telefon**	The phone
Kapı	The door	**Masa**	Table
Çekmece	The drawer	**Buzdolabı**	The fridge
Şifoniyer	The dresser	**Yastık**	The pillow
DVD oynatıcı	DVD player	**Tablo**	Table
kat / üst kat	The floor / upstairs	**Çatı**	The roof
Saat	The clock	**Duş**	The shower
Dolap	Closet	**Oda**	The room

Bilgisayar	The computer	lavabo / lavabo	Sink / washbasin
Köşe	The corner	Kanepe	The couch
Kütüphane	The library	Merdivenler	The staircase
Halı	The carpet	Soba	The stove
Tavan	The ceiling	Dokunmak	Tap
Sandalye	The chair	Raf	The shelf
Şömine	The fireplace		

Clothing, accessories and beauty products (Giyim, aksesuar ve güzellik ürünleri)

Bornoz	Bathrobe	oje çıkarıcı	Remover
Gömlek	Shirt	Eşarp	Scarf
Ayakkabı	Shoe	Bilezik	Bracelet
ayakkabı bağı	Lace	Fırça	Brush
Şort	Short	Lens	Lens
Etek	Skirt	saç spreyi	Hair spray
Cep	Poached	Tarak	Comb
Pijama	Pajamas	Sampuan	Shampoo
el çantası	Handbag	Yüzük	Ring
Eldivenler	Gloves	göz kalemi	Eyeliner
Küpe	Earring	göz farı	Eye shadow
Kulaklıklar	Earphones	Gözlük	Glasses
Elbise	Bathrobe	Saç kurutma makinesi	Hair dryer
Yaka	Coal	Mendil	Tissue
Ceket	Jacket	Losyon	Lotion
Şapka	Hat	Ruj	Lipstick

Sutyen	Bra	Makyaj	Makeup
Bluz	Blouse	Ustura	The razor
Kemer	Belt	Pudra	Powder
Terlik	Slipper	toplu iğne	Pin
Yağmurluk	Raincoat	Parfum	Perfume
Kol	Sleeves	Kolye	Necklace
Pantolon	Trousers	Rimel	Mascara
Sandalet	Sandals	tırnak makası	Nail clipper
iç çamaşırı	Underwear	tırnak törpüsü	Nail file
Tişört	T-shirt	tırnak cilası	Nail polish
Çorap	Socks		
Mayo	Swimsuit		
Tenis ayakkabıları	Tennis shoes		

Work (işler)

Muhasebeci	Accountant	Duvarcı	Mason
aktör / aktris	The actor / actress	Mekanik	The mechanic
Mimar	The architect	Model	The model
Yazar	The writer	Müzisyen	The musician
Fırıncı	The Baker	Hemşire	The nurse
kitap dükkanı	The bookstore	Memur	The officer
Tüccar	The merchant	Göz doktoru	Ophthalmologist
Kasap	The butcher	Gözlükçü	The optician
Resmi	The official	Ressam	The painter
Programcı	Programmer	Çocuk doktoru	The pediatrician

Pişirici	Cook	**Kimyager**	The chemist
Müşteri	The customer	**Fotoğraf**	The photograph
Dişçi	The dentist	**Tesisatçı**	The plumber
Doktor	Doctor	**Polis**	The policeman
Elektrikçi	Electrician	**Postacı**	The postman
Çalışan	The employee	**Rahip**	The priest
kütüphaneci	Librarian	**Öğrenci**	The student
Avukat	Avocado	**Sarkıcı**	The singer
Yargıç	The judge	**Asker**	The soldier
Gazeteci	The journalist	**Ayakkabıcı**	The shoemaker
Kuyumcu	Jeweler	**Garson**	The waiter / waitress
Kuaför	The hairdresser	**Öğretmen (lise)**	The teacher (high school)
Bakkal	The grocer	**Terzi**	The tailor
Bahçıvan	The gardener	**Cerrah**	The surgeon
Mühendis	The engineer	**Öğretmen (üniversite)**	The professor (the university)
işçi (fabrika)	The worker (factory)	**Editör**	Editor
İtfaiyeci	The fireman	**Satıcı**	Seller
Balıkçı	The fisherman	**Bilim insanı**	The scientist
Görevli	The steward	**Sekreter**	The Secretary

Sports, games and recreation

Atletizm	Athleticism	**Tenis**	Tennis

Yüzme	Swimming	**Filmleri izlemek**	Watch the movies
masa Tenisi	Ping pong	**Kestirmek**	Take a nap
Beyzbol	Athleticism	**Voleybol su kayağı**	Volleyball
Basketbol	Basketball	**Güreş / güreş**	Water skiing
Bowling	Bowling	**Başarısızlıklar**	Wrestling / wrestling
Boks	Boxing	**Dama oyunu**	checkers game
Kros kayağı	Cross-country skiing	**Kartlar**	The cards
bisiklet sürmek	Cycling	**Poker**	Poker
Yokuş aşağı kayak	Downhill skiing	**Masa oyunları**	Board games
Amerikan futbolu	American Football	**Video oyunları**	Video games
Golf	Golf	**Dartlar**	The darts
Doğa yürüyüşü	Hiking	**Domino**	Dominoes
Hokey	Hockey	**Kamp yapmak**	Camping
Ata binme	The horse riding	**Rafting**	Rafting
Buz pateni	The ice skating	**Dikiş**	Sewing
Koşu yapmak	Jogging	**Bahçıvanlık**	Gardening
Paten	Rollerblading	**Fotoğrafçılık**	Photography

Tekerlekli patenle kaymak	Roller skating	**Boyama**	The painting
Futbol	Football	**Örme**	Knitting
Sörf	Surf	**Bulmacalar**	Puzzles
Ragbi	Rugby	**Çizim**	The drawing
Yelken	Sailing	**Doğrama işleri**	Woodwork
		Çanak çömlek	Pottery

Nature

Bulut	The cloud	**Yarımada**	The peninsula
Hava	The air	**Düz**	The plain
Kıyı	The shore	**düşük gelgit**	Low tide
Sahil	The beach	**Ay**	The moon
Sube	Branch	**Dağ**	The mountain
Köprü	The bridge	**Dağ silsilesi**	The mountain range
Düğme	The button	**Ağız**	Mouthpiece
Sehir	The city	**Gölge**	The shadow
Mağara	Cave	**Deniz**	The sea
Karanlık	Darkness	**Kum**	Sand
Çiy	The dew	**Gül**	The Rose
Papatya	Daisy	**Kök**	The root
Ülke	The country	**Kaya**	The rock
Sahil	The coast	**Nehir**	The river
Çalılık	The Bush	**Gökkuşağı**	The Rainbow
Nergis	Daffodil	**Yağmur**	The rain

Akış	The stream	Gölet	The pond
Kırsal yer	The countryside	Bitki	The plant
Takımyıldız	The constellation	Gezegen	The planet
kuyruklu yıldız	Comet	Kaynak	Source
Çöl	The desert	Yıldız	The star
Gökyüzü	The sky	Çubuk	The rod
Toz	Dust	Fırtına	The storm
Dünya	World	Boğaz	The strait
Çiftlik	The farm	Akış	The stream
Alan	Field	Ayçiçeği	The sunflower
Yeşillik	Foliage	Gök gürültüsü	Thunder
Orman	The forest	Kasırga	The tornado
Jöle	The jelly	Ağaç	The tree
Çimen	The grass	Gövde	Trunk
Yüksek gelgit	High tide	Temiz su	Freshwater
Vadi	The valley	Görünüm	View
Tepe	The hill	Su	The water
Buz	Ice	tuzlu su	Salted water
Orman	The jungle	Şelale	The waterfall
Göl	Lake	dalga / dalga	The wave / the wave
Yaprak	Leaf	Zaman	Time
Işık	The light	Rüzgar	Wind
Şimşe	Lightning	Dünya	The world
Ada	The island		

Foods and meals (gidalar ve yemek)

Kahve	Coffee	**Sebze**	The vegetable
domuz pastırması	Bacon	**Sos**	The sauce
sığır eti	Beef	**Sosis**	The sausage
Bira	Beer	**Meşrubat**	Soft drink
Içecek	The beverage	**Çorba**	Soup
Ekmek	The bread	**taze / ekşi krema**	Sour cream / sour cream
Kahvaltı	Breakfast	**Biftek**	The steak
Bisküvi	The biscuit	**Güveç**	Stew
Tereyağı	Butter	**Şeker**	Sugar
Kek	The cake	**Lokanta**	The diner
Seker	The candy	**Çay**	Tea
Peynir	Cheese	**tost / tost**	Toast / toast
Çikolata	Chocolate	**Türkiye**	Turkey
Tavuk	The chicken	**Buzağı**	Calf
Yemek	The meal	**Tava**	Pan
öğle yemeği	Lunch	**Çatal**	The fork
meyve suyu	The juice	**Tabak**	The dish, the plate
Reçel	Jam	**Kupa**	The mug
Buz	Ice	**Tirbuşon**	The corkscrew
Bal	Honey	**Kevgir**	Colander
Hamburger	The hamburger	**kahve makinesi**	The coffee maker
Jambon	Ham	**Çin yemek çubukları**	Chinese chopsticks
Meyve	Fruit	**yogurt**	Yogurt
Un	Flour	**Çanta**	The bag
süzme peynir	White cheese	**Kase**	The bowl

bisküvi / kurabiye	The biscuit / cookie	**Şişe**	The bottle
pamuk şeker	Cotton candy	**kutu / karton**	Box / carton
Krem	Cream	**konserve açacağı**	Can opener
Muhallebi	English cream	**Sandviç**	The sandwich
Tatlı	Dessert	**Sirke**	The vinegar
akşam yemegi	Dinner	**Su**	The water
Yumurta	The egg	**krem şanti**	Whipped cream
Sişman	The fat	**Şarap**	Wine
Et	Meat	**Bardak**	Glass
Süt	Milk	**kavanoz / kavanoz**	The jar / the jar
Hardal	The mustard	**Sürahi**	The pitcher
sıvı yağ	Oil	**su ısıtıcı**	Kettle
Omlet	Omelet	**Bıçak**	The knife
Biber	The pepper	**Kapak**	Lid
Turta	The pie	**Peçete**	The napkin
domuz eti	Pork	**Tabak**	The plate
tatlı krema	The serving cream	**Fincan tabağı**	Saucer
Pirinç	Rice	**Tava**	The pan
Kızartma	The roast	**Kaşık**	The spoon
küçük ekmek	The little bread	**Bomba**	The bomb
Salata	The salad	**Masa**	Table
Salam	Salami	**Masa örtüsü**	The tablecloth
Tuz	Salt	**Çaydanlık**	The teapot

Animals

Hayvan	Animal	lamba	Lamb
Karınca	The ant	tarla kuşu	The lark
Antilop	Antelope	Aslan	Lion
Anten	Antenna	kertenkele	The lizard
Boynuzlar	Antlers	Istakoz	Lobster
Porsuk	The badger	bit (bit)	The louse (lice)
Yarasa	The bat	orkinos	Mackerel
Gaga	Beak	köstebek	The mole
Ayı	Bear	maymun	The monkey
Arı	The bee	sivrisinek	Mosquito
Bokböceği	The scarab	güve	The moth
Kuş	The bird	fare fareler)	The mouse (the mice)
Robin	Robin	katır	The mule
Boğa	The bull	midye	The mussel
Kelebek	The butterfly	yuva	The nest
Dana eti	The veal	Bülbül	The Nightingale
Sazan	Carp	ahtapot	The octopus
Kedi	Cat	devekuşu	Ostrich
Tırtıl	The caterpillar	baykuş	The owl
Çita	Cheetah	öküz (öküz)	Beef (oxen)
Tavuk	The chicken	istiridye	Oyster
Şempanze	The chimpanzee	papağan	The parrot
Pençe	The claw	keklik	Partridge
Hamamböceği	The cockroach	pençe	The paw
Morina	Cod	Penguen	The Penguin
Koza	The cocoon	domuz	The pig

İnek	The cow	güvercin	Pigeon
Yengeç	The crab	turna balığı	The pike
Kerevit	Crayfish	midilli	The pony
Timsah	The crocodile	tavşan	The rabbit
Karga	The crow	rakun	The raccoon
Geyik	The deer / s	sıçan	The rat
Köpek	The dog	horoz	Rooster
Eşek	Donkey	somon balığı	The salmon
Yusufçuk	The dragonfly	ölcek	The scale
Ördek	Duck	Akrep	The Scorpion
Kartal	The Eagle	Martı	The Seagull
Yılanbalığı	Eel	denizatı	The seahorse
Yumurta	The egg	mühür	Seal
Fil	Elephant	köpekbalığı	The shark
kuş tüyü	Feather	koyun	The sheep
Yüzgeç	The fin	karides	The shrimp
Balık	Fish	cilt	The skin
Çip	The chip	Sülük	Slug
Uçmak	Fly	salyangoz	The snail
Tilki	Fox	yılan	The snake
Kurbağa	Frog	serçe	The Sparrow
Kürk	Fur	örümcek	The spider
Solungaç	The gill	kalamar	Squid
GIRAFE	The GIRAFE	Sincap	The squirrel
Keçi	The goat	denizyıldızı	The starfish
kaz (kaz)	Goose (geese)	leylek	The stork
Goril	The gorilla	Yutmak	The swallow
Çekirge	The grasshopper	kuğu	The Swan
Hamster	The hamster	kurbağa yavrusu	The tadpole
Tavşan	Hare	kuyruk	Tail

Kirpi	The Hedgehog	Kaplan	The Tiger
Tavuk	The hen	kurbağa	The toad
Yusufçuk	The dragonfly	ölcek	The scale
Ördek	Duck	Akrep	The Scorpion
Kartal	The Eagle	Martı	The Seagull
Yılanbalığı	Eel	denizatı	The seahorse
Yumurta	The egg	mühür	Seal
Fil	Elephant	köpekbalığı	The shark
kuş tüyü	Feather	koyun	The sheep
Yüzgeç	The fin	karides	The shrimp
Balık	Fish	cilt	The skin
Çip	The chip	Sülük	Slug
Uçmak	Fly	salyangoz	The snail
Tilki	Fox	yılan	The snake

Countries and nationalities

Afrika	Africa	İrlanda	Ireland
Afrikalı	African	İrlandalı	Irish
Arnavutluk	Albania	İsrail	Israel
Arnavut	Albanian	İsrailli	Israeli
Amerika	America	İtalya	Italy
Amerikalı	American	İtalyan	Italian
Arjantin	Argentina	Japonya	Japan
Arjantinli	Argentine	Japon	Japanese
Asya	Asia	Letonya	Latvia
Asyalı	Asian	Leton	Latvian
Avustralya	Australia	litvanya	Lithuania
Avustralyalı	Australian	Litvanyalı	Lithuanian
Avusturya	Austria	Lüksemburg	Luxembourg

Avusturyalı	Austrian	**Lüksemburglu**	Luxembourgish
Belçika	Belgium	**Malta**	Malta
Belçikalı	Belgian	**Maltalı**	Maltese
Bosna	Bosnia	**Hollanda**	Netherlands
Bosnalı	Bosnian	**hollandalı**	Dutch
Brezilya	Brazil	**Yeni Zelanda**	New Zealand
Brezilyalı	Brazilian	**Yeni Zelandalı**	New Zealand
Bulgaristan	Bulgaria	**Norveç**	Norway
Bulgar	Bulgarian	**Norveçli**	Norwegian
Kanada	Canada	**Makedonya**	Macedonia
Kanadalı	Canadian	**Makedonyalı**	Macedonian
Çin	China	**Meksika**	Mexico
Çinli	Chinese	**Meksikalı**	Mexican
Danimarka	Croatia	**Romanya**	Romania
Danimarka dili	Croatian	**Romence**	Romanian
Mısır	Egypt	**Rusya**	Russia
Mısırlı	Egyptian	**Rus**	Russian
İngiltere	England	**İskoçya**	Scotland
ingiliz	British	**İskoç**	Scottish
Estonya	Estonia	**Sırbistan**	Serbia
Estonyalı	Estonian	**Sırp**	Serbian
Avrupa	Europe	**Slovakya**	Slovakia
Avrupalı	European	**Slovak**	Slovak
Finlandiya	Finland	**Slovenya**	Slovenia
Finli	Finnish	**Sloven**	Slovenian
Fransa	France	**ispanya**	Spain
Fransız	French	**İspanyol**	Spanish
Almanya	Germany	**İsveç**	Sweden
Almanlı	German	**İsveçli**	Swedish
Büyük Britanya	Great Britain	**İsviçre**	Switzerland
ingiliz	British	**İsviçre**	Swiss

Yunanistan	Greece	Türkiye	Turkey
yunan / yunan	Greek	türk / türk	Turkish
Macaristan	Hungary	Ukrayna	Ukraine
Macar	Hungarian	Ukraynalı	Ukrainian
İzlanda	Iceland	Birleşik Krallık	The United Kingdom
İzlandalı	Icelandic	Amerika Birleşik Devletleri	United States

3 *Practice*

3.1 Text: İki kardeş

Erkek kardeşlerin ikisi de babalarında kalma çiftlikte çalışırlardı. Kardeşlerden biri evliydi ve çok çocuğu vardı. Diğeri ise bekardı. Her günün sonunda iki erkek kardeş ürünlerini ve kârlarını eşit olarak bölüsürlerdi.

Günün birinde bekar kardeş kendi kendine :

" Ürünümüzü ve kârmızı eşit olarak bölüşmemiz hiç de hakça değil" dedi, "ben yalnızım ve pek fazla ihtiyacım yok. Böylelikle, her gece evinden çıkıp, bir çuval tahılı gizlice erkek kardeşinin evindeki tahıl deposuna götürmeye başladı. Bu arada evil olan kardeş, kendi kendine:

" Ürünümüzü ve kârmızı eşit olarak bölüşmemiz hiç de hakça degil, üstelik ben evliyim, bir eşim ve çocuklarım var ve yaslandığım zaman onlar bana bakabilirler. Oysa kardeşimin kimsesi yok, yaslandığı zaman hiç kimsesi yok bakacak" diyordu.

Böylece evli olan kardeş her gece evinden cıkıp, bir çuval tahılı gizlice erkek kardeşinin tahıl deposuna götürmeye basladı. Iki kardes de yıllarca ne olup bittiğini bir türlü anlayamadılar, çünkü her ikisinin de deposundaki tahılın miktarı değişmiyordu. Sonra,

bir gece iki kardeş gizlice birbirlerinin deposuna tahıl tasırken çarpısıverdiler. O anda olan biteni anladılar. Çuvallarini yere birakip birbirlerini kucakladilar.

Hayattaki en yüce mutluluk, sevildigimize inanmaktir.[3]

Read the text several times to improve your reading of the Turkish language. Locate the words you recognize, the cases, the suffixes, the verbs, ...Study the text to try to understand it.

3.2 Conversation

L: *Merhaba, nasılsınız?*	Hi, how are you ?
M: *İyiyim. Ya sen ?*	I'm good, and you?
L: *Ben de çok iyiyim.*	I'm also good.
M: *Adın ne ?*	what's your name?
L: *Benim adım Laura, siz adınız ne?*	My name's Laure, and you?
M: *Ben Mehmet.*	I'm Mehmet.
L: *Tanıştığıma memnun oldum*	nice to meet you!
M: *Ben de memnun oldum.*	nice to meet you too!
L: *Kaç yaşındasınız Mehmet Abi?*	How old are you, Big brother Mehmet?
M: *Ben 35 yaşındayım. Sen ?*	I'm 35 years old, and you?
L: *16 yaşındayım.*	I'm 16.
M: *Nerelisin?*	Where are you fom?
L: *Fransızım. Ya siz ?*	I'm from France, and You?
M: *Ben türküm*	I'm from Turkey (I'm turkish).
L: *Nerede yaşıyorsunuz?*	Where do you live?
M: *Annecy'de yaşıyorum.*	I live in Annecy.

---

[3] Hacettepe University. (). *Kardesilik böyle olur.* Available: http://yunus.hacettepe.edu.tr/~b0123213/kardeslik_boyle_olur. htm. Last accessed 28th sept 2020.

Ne iş yapıyorsun?	What job do you do?
L: Öğrenciyim.	I am a student.
M: Ah çok güzel. üniversitede ne okuyorsun?	Ah that's good. What do you study?
L: İşletme	business
M: Hangi yıldasın	in which year are you in?
L: 2. sınıftayım	I'm in 2nd year.
Siz ne iş yapıyorsunuz?	*And you, what do you do?*
M: Ögretmenim	*I'm a teacher!*
L: Ne öğretiyorsun ?	*what do you teach?*
M: Dünya Tarihi	*world history.*
Erkek ve kız kardeşlerin var mı?	*do you have brothers and sisters?*
L: Bir erkek kardeşim ve iki kız kardeşim var. siz?	I have one brother and two sisters. And you?
M: Ben tek çocuğum.	I'm the only son.
Evcil hayvanın var mı?	Do you have pets?
L: Evet.Bir kedim / köpeğim / hamsterim var.	I have a cat, a dog and a hamster.
M: Köpekleri sevmiyorum.	I don't love dogs.
L: Neden ?	why?
M: Çünkü çok havlıyorlar	because they bark too much.
L : Spor yapıyor musun ?	do you pratice any sport?
M: Evet.	Yes!
L: Hangısı ?	which one?
M: Futbol, tenis ve basketbol oynuyorum	I plan Football, Tennis and basketball.
M: iyi türkçe konuşuyorsun. türkçeyi nerden öğrendin?	You speak Turkish very well, where did you learn from?

L: *Bana öğreten bir arkadaşım var* *I have a friend who teaches me.*

M: *erkek arkadaşın mı?* İs he you boyfriend?

L: *neden soruyorsun ?* why you do ask?

M: *boşver !* never mind!

L: *annem beni bekliyor. Gitmek zorundayım.* My mother's waiting for me. I have to go.

M: *Tamam ! git ! Güle güle.* Ok. Go. Bye!

L: *Teşekkür ederim. Yakında görüşürüz.* Thank you. See you soon!

4 Conclusion and advices

Learning a new thing isn't the easiest, but it's opening up to a whole new culture, a whole new way of doing things, a new world.

For English speakers, Turkish is not easy to learn, but it is not impossible either. Once we immerse ourselves in the Turkish language, we realize that it is a language like any other and it can be learned.

If you are holding this booklet in your hands, it is because you really want to learn Turkish, so here are some tips for you:

1. Find a language partner, preferably a native Turkish speaker.

2. Practice a lot with him

3. Build up your vocabulary.

"Studying another language is not only learning other words to mean the same things, but also learning another way of thinking about those things" - Flora Lewis

Ben — I am
Sen — you
memnum oldum — nice to meet you
Hoşça kalın — Bye

Printed in Great Britain
by Amazon